DREW BREES

SUPERSTAR QUARTERBACK

BIG BUDDY NFL SUPERSTARS

Big Buddy Books
An Imprint of Abdo Publishing
abdobooks.com

DENNIS ST. SAUVER

abdobooks.com

Published by Abdo Publishing, a division of ABDO, PO Box 398166, Minneapolis, Minnesota 55439.

Big Buddy Books™ is a trademark and logo of Abdo Publishing.

Printed in the United States of America, North Mankato, Minnesota.
052019
092019

Cover Photo: efks/Getty Images; Jonathan Bachman/Getty Images.
Interior Photos: Andy Kropa/Getty Images (p. 19); Chip Somodevilla/Getty Images (p. 27); Cynthia Lum/Getty Images (p. 9); Doug Benc/Getty Images (p. 21); Harry How/Getty Images (pp. 23, 29); Lee Celano/Getty Images (p. 25); Robert B. Stanton/Getty Images (p. 17); Stephen Dunn/Getty Images (p. 15); Suzanne Plunkett/AP Images (p. 13); Tom Strattman/AP Images (p. 11); Wesley Hitt/Getty Images (p. 5).

Coordinating Series Editor: Elizabeth Andrews
Graphic Design: Jenny Christensen, Cody Laberda

Library of Congress Control Number: 2018967162

Publisher's Cataloging-in-Publication Data

Names: St. Sauver, Dennis, author.
Title: Drew Brees: superstar quarterback / by Dennis St. Sauver
Other title: Superstar quarterback
Description: Minneapolis, Minnesota : Abdo Publishing, 2020 | Series: NFL superstars | Includes online resources and index.
Identifiers: ISBN 9781532119798 (lib. bdg.) | ISBN 9781532174551 (ebook)
Subjects: LCSH: Brees, Drew, 1979- --Juvenile literature. | Football players--United States--Biography--Juvenile literature. | Quarterbacks (Football)--United States--Biography--Juvenile literature. | New Orleans Saints (Football team)--Juvenile literature.
Classification: DDC 796.3326409 [B]--dc23

CONTENTS

SUPERSTAR QUARTERBACK

Drew Brees is one of the top quarterbacks in the National Football League (NFL). He plays for the New Orleans Saints in Louisiana.

After a successful 2009 season, Drew led the Saints to victory in the Super Bowl. He was then named the Super Bowl **Most Valuable Player (MVP)**.

SNAPSHOT

NAME:
Andrew Christopher Brees

BIRTHDAY:
January 15, 1979

BIRTHPLACE:
Austin, Texas

POSITION:
Quarterback

COLLEGE TEAM:
Purdue University Boilermakers

PAST NFL TEAM:
San Diego Chargers

CURRENT TEAM:
New Orleans Saints

EARLY YEARS

Drew was born in Austin, Texas. His parents are Eugene and Mina Brees. His brother Reid is two years younger than Drew. The two are very close friends.

Both of Drew's parents were good at sports. Eugene played basketball in college. Mina was a star in three sports in high school.

DID YOU KNOW?

Drew's uncle Marty Akins was a star quarterback in college during the 1970s. He played for the University of Texas Longhorns.

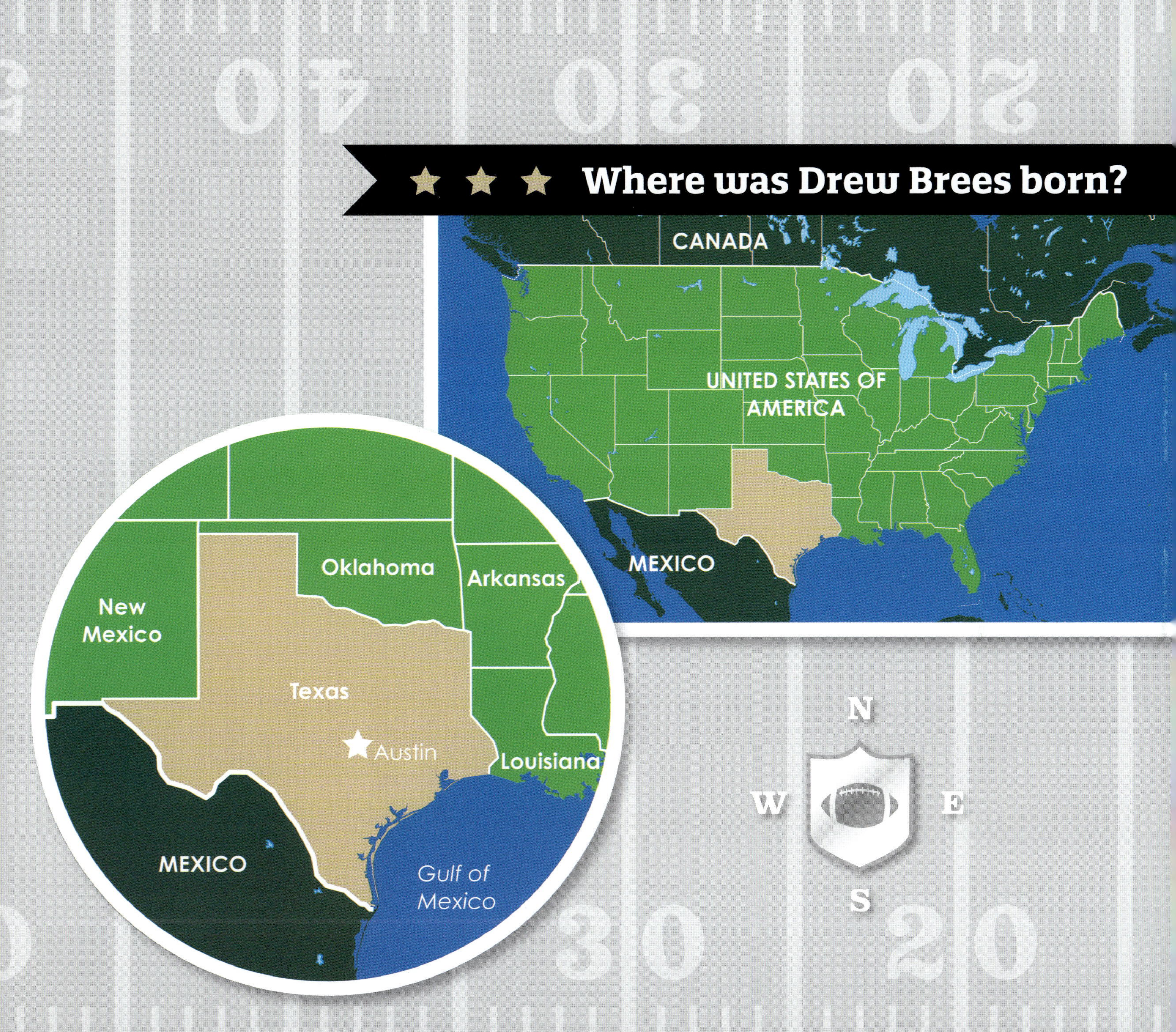
Where was Drew Brees born?
CANADA
UNITED STATES OF AMERICA
MEXICO
New Mexico
Oklahoma
Arkansas
Texas
Austin
Louisiana
MEXICO
Gulf of Mexico
N
W
E
S

STARTING OUT

Like many **professional** athletes, Drew was good at many sports growing up. He played baseball, basketball, and football at Westlake High School in Austin. There, he really shined on the football field.

During his senior year, Drew's team won the 1996 Texas 5A **Championship**. Drew was named the Offensive Player of the Year.

Drew was one of the top youth tennis players in Texas. He even played against professional tennis player Andy Roddick *(right)*!

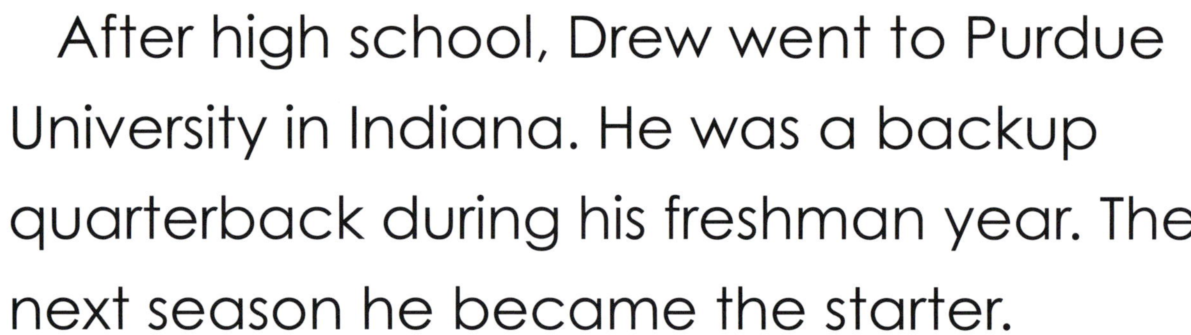

After high school, Drew went to Purdue University in Indiana. He was a backup quarterback during his freshman year. The next season he became the starter.

During his four years in college, Drew led his team to a Big Ten **Championship**. He still leads the Big Ten **Conference** in **passing** yards. Drew threw for 11,792 yards (10,782 m) for the Purdue Boilermakers.

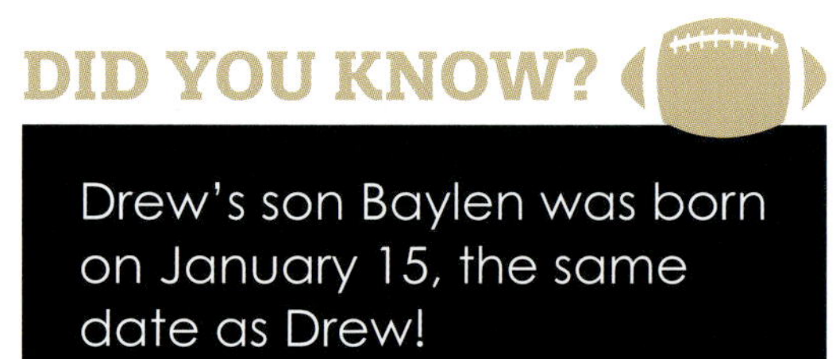

DID YOU KNOW?

Drew's son Baylen was born on January 15, the same date as Drew!

At the end of the 2000 season, Purdue made it to the Rose Bowl in California. Sadly, the team lost to the Washington Huskies.

BIG DREAMS

In college, Drew was a very good student. He was an Academic **All-American** in 2000.

He continued to play hard on the field as well. Drew won the Maxwell Award as the nation's top college player in 2000. He was also in the running for the **Heisman Trophy** two times. Drew set many records for Purdue in college, and the NFL noticed.

Drew *(left)*, Chris Weinke *(center)*, and LaDainian Tomlinson *(right)* were three of the players competing for the Heisman Trophy in 2000.

GOING PRO

In 2001, Drew was the thirty-second pick in the NFL **draft**. The San Diego Chargers selected him.

As a Charger, Drew proved to be one of the NFL's best quarterbacks. He stepped in to become the starter for San Diego in 2002. He led the team to the 2004 season **playoffs**.

Drew wore number nine on his jersey when he played for the Chargers. He still plays as number nine for the Saints.

Drew was **second-string** quarterback for his first seven games with the Chargers. But he took over after the starting quarterback was hurt in a game.

Drew threw his first touchdown in that game. He almost led the team to victory after being 20 points behind. Drew had proven himself a strong player.

Drew has been called a gunslinger. That is because he throws hard, exact passes to his wide receivers.

A RISING STAR

In 2004, Drew had a great season. He had one of the highest quarterback ratings in the league. He led the Chargers to the AFC West **Championship** for the first time in ten seasons.

In 2006, Drew chose to play with the New Orleans Saints. Soon after, he led his new team to a Super Bowl victory. He earned the game's **MVP** honors.

Sports Illustrated named Drew the 2010 Sportsman of the Year.

Drew continued to improve during his time with the Saints. He set an NFL record with 5,476 **passing** yards (5,007 m) in 2011. That same year, he threw 46 touchdowns.

Drew is the all-time passing leader for the Saints. He has passed for more than 62,000 yards (56,693 m) and nearly 450 touchdowns! Drew has led the Saints to the **playoffs** six times.

The Saints won 13 out of 16 games in 2009. With Drew's help, the team went on to win the Super Bowl!

OFF THE FIELD

Drew and his wife Brittany have four children. They have three sons named Baylen, Bowen, and Callen. And they have one daughter named Rylen.

Drew wrote a very popular book in 2010 called *Coming Back Stronger*. It is about his **ability** to continue playing after going through tough times.

Drew loves hanging out with his family during his free time. They especially enjoy celebrating birthdays together.

GIVING BACK

Drew and Brittany are very kind. They **donate** money to Purdue for education and athletics.

The couple started the Brees Dream **Foundation** in 2003. With many other partners, the foundation has raised more than $25 million. The money helps people who have **cancer**.

Operation Kids is another foundation that the Brees family supports. It helps to rebuild parks and playgrounds, and fund after-school programs for kids.

AWARDS

Drew has won many awards during his football **career**. He has been named to the **Pro Bowl** 11 times.

In 2006, he received the NFL Walter Payton Man of the Year Award. He also won the 2008 and 2011 NFL Offensive Player of the Year awards. In 2010, the Associated Press named Drew the Male Athlete of the Year.

In 2010, Drew became part of Barack Obama's President's Council. It was called Fitness, Sports, and Nutrition.

BUZZ

Drew became the NFL's all-time leading **passer** in 2018. He broke Peyton Manning's record. The new record is 74,437 yards (68,065 m). And his **career** is not even finished!

Drew has been asked if he might enter **politics** when he leaves the NFL. He has not decided, but he is thinking about it.

Drew has been very helpful to the people of New Orleans since Hurricane Katrina in 2005.

GLOSSARY

ability the power to do something.

All-American selected as one of the best in the US in a particular sport.

cancer any of a group of very harmful diseases that cause a body's cells to become unhealthy.

career a period of time spent in a certain job.

championship a game, a match, or a race held to find a first-place winner.

conference a group of sports teams that play against each other and that are part of a larger league of teams.

donate giving something to help those in need.

draft a system for professional sports teams to choose new players.

foundation (faun-DAY-shuhn) an organization that controls gifts of money and services.

Heisman Trophy (HAIS-muhn TROH-fee) an award given each year to the most outstanding player in college football.

Most Valuable Player (MVP) the player who contributes the most to his or her team's success.

pass to throw the football in the direction of the opponent's goal.

playoffs a game or series of games to determine a championship or break a tie.

Pro Bowl a game that features the best players in the NFL. It does not count toward regular-season records.

politics the art or science of government.

professional (pruh-FEHSH-nuhl) paid to do a sport or activity.

second-string someone who is not used as one of the regular players on a team.

ONLINE RESOURCES

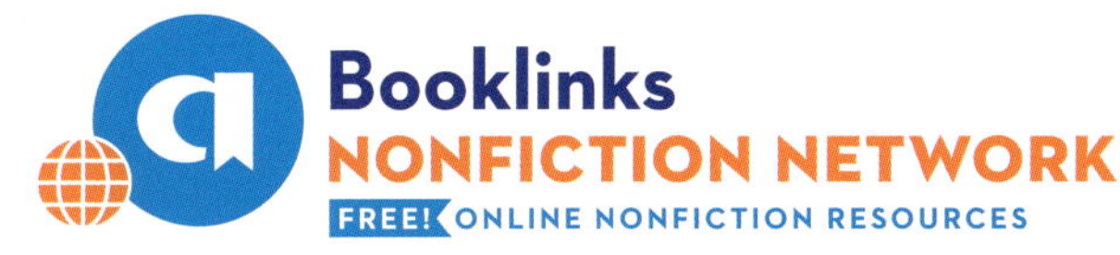

To learn more about Drew Brees, please visit **abdobooklinks.com** or scan this QR code. These links are routinely monitored and updated to provide the most current information available.

★ ★ ★ INDEX ★ ★ ★